# THE CANADIAN BRASS

## Book of easy quintets
### *With discussion and techniques*

By WALTER H. BARNES

Arranged for:
1st (B♭) Trumpet
2nd (B♭) Trumpet
Horn in F
Trombone
Tuba
→ Conductor

# THE CANADIAN BRASS EDUCATIONAL SERIES

DISTRIBUTED BY

HAL•LEONARD®
CORPORATION

7777 W. BLUEMOUND RD. P.O. BOX 13819 MILWAUKEE, WI 53213

# THE CANADIAN BRASS

## Book of easy quintets
## With discussion and techniques

By WALTER H. BARNES

# Contents

| | | | | Page |
|---|---|---|---|---|
| 1 | Hosanna | Palestrina | E | 11 |
| 2 | Non Nobis Domine (Canon) | Byrd | E | 11 |
| 3 | The Silver Swan | Gibbons | M | 13 |
| 4 | Intrada – A Fanfare | Pezel | E | 15 |
| 5 | Fugue in E$^b$ | Bach | M | 17 |
| 6 | Air (from Water Music) | Handel | D | 19 |
| 7 | Ave Verum | Mozart | M | 23 |
| 8 | Ave Maria | Rachmaninoff | D | 27 |
| 9 | Cwm Rhondda | Welsh | E | 29 |
| 10 | Carol of the Bells | Ukrainian | M | 31 |
| 11 | El Yivneh Hagalil | Israel | M | 35 |
| 12 | Bones | Spiritual | D | 36 |
| 13 | Three Newfoundland Folksongs | Canadian | M | 39 |
| 14 | The Lord Bless You & Keep You | American | M | 40 |
| 15 | My Country, 'Tis of Thee/ God Save the Queen | | E | 41 |
| 16 | O Canada | Lavallée | M | 42 |

E  Easy        M  Medium        D  Difficult

# A 'note' to you (T.B.T.)

Ensemble playing is one of the great rewards of Instrumental Music. YOU ARE IMPORTANT!!! You cannot be 'covered', or your sound hidden. You stand on your own, with your musical friends needing you as you need them. As you progress through our book, you become a better listener as well as a better performer. All your other musical groups (bands, orchestras) benefit from your experience here. But, most of all, this ensemble book introduces you to a new world of musical enjoyment and equal participation.

We want to stress three basics: **Tone, Balance, and Tuning**

Music is different from all other Art forms in that sound is more important than what is seen. Your *Tone* should be free-flowing, sitting on the air column with ease, round, well-focused, and able to blend with your ensemble. You must always listen to yourself and concern yourself with the best sound that you can make.

Now, bring your tone to your ensemble and realize that the political phrase of Equality has never been truer. You must be an equal part of your small group, not more — not less. *Balance* your sound by listening to the others. At times you will have the melody or the projecting part; your friends will support you. Other times will require that you support your partners. This is done by listening and balancing your part in an equal but changeable relation to the whole sound.

Equality has its foundation in relationship to others. So does *Tuning*. You must listen all around you, but especially to your foundation — the Tuba or the lowest instrument playing at the time. If you are the Tuba player, you must be very careful to place each note in tune so that you provide a consistent foundation for the others. Before you begin performing, tune your instruments together on a concert B♭. Then, play the last note of the piece and fit into the chord. Your note will have a proper place that helps the chord shine. The secret is — careful listening in a musical relationship with your friends. We suggest that you acquire from your music store, the cassette tape (recorded by us) of the music in this book.

Most of the selections that we have arranged here were purposely chosen from Choral literature! But take heart and heed, fellow Brass players. Choral music is the marriage of word and note phrases making music sentences and, collectively, sound paragraphs. Inherent in a successful presentation is the punctuation — breathing marks. We have carefully marked each selection so that you are better able to 'sing' each phrase, supporting your sound with an intensity of air column for your tonal production. Follow these breathmarks (') as an indication of phrases.

We have only marked the basic dynamics. We hope that you (with the entire group), after learning the notes and phrases, will develop *your own* interpretation, and therefore your own volume markings. (We have provided 'tempo' suggestions.) Your creativity, rather than the imposition of our interpretation, will enable your ensemble to grow together musically.

Have fun!

Canadian Brass

# To the music teacher

Dear Educator:

We know well from our experience the enormous task you have as a teacher of performance music. Besides your regular classes, planning, fund-raising, repairing, ordering materials, concerts, etc., you realize the important need of small ensemble groups for musical and social development of your students.

But, where's the time and energy?

We have developed an interesting and innovative approach for Brass Ensembles. This book is a collection of fine selections supported by our personal comments and suggestions to your students. It's *almost* a self-help method. Dynamic marks are included but not in great detail. We hope that the performers will collectively come to musical decisions which will help them to grow creatively, while still relying on you for mature and experienced judgement. Meanwhile, they should be able to progress somewhat on their own, following our comments and suggestions, leaving you freer for your many other tasks, yet accomplishing for them another facet of Music Education.

Our book encompasses several centuries of music, largely from the Choral idiom, but suited to a Brass Quintet or Ensemble. (Don't be afraid of doubling parts; the younger less-experienced player might need the confidence and support of another player on his line.) We have stressed musical phrases through breathing; tone, tuning and balance are discussed in detail, and become more important through the polyphony presented. We have kept equality of instruments in mind: the Tuba line is not just a rhythmic part; the second trumpet part is not just 'harmonic fill'; we have kept the second part in a more limited range, but strongly suggest that you alternate Trumpet players so that *both* learn to play and hear an inner part — so important for tuning. We have presented music that helps develop the specific characteristics of the individual members of the Brass family. We have kept to a suitable range and choice of keys in our planning for the inexperienced player. And our Book represents a variety of selections to satisfy the needs of your students without involving them in music too difficult to prepare for performance within a reasonably short period.

#1-14 is generally both chronological and technically progressive, though we do include 'standard of difficulty' with your Table of Contents.

Finally, we believe that we have produced a unique Anthology-Method book suitable for the vast numbers of Brass Ensembles that are forming in Elementary and Secondary Music programmes. We sincerely hope that our efforts will serve you and your students.

*Canadian Brass*
*Walter H. Barnes*
*(editor & teacher)*

Note: You will find space allowed in our unique layout for the teacher or conductor to make performance suggestions.

# Warm-up

**Editor**  Gentlemen. Could we have a discussion on the very important area of warm-up. I see so many students who literally 'grab' their instrument out of their case and begin playing. What do *you* do?

**Tuba**  The first thing I do is play a long single note on the mouthpiece. That's to loosen up the lips and find pitch through the middle of the air column. Then, try a very simple four-note mouthpiece warm-up for a minute or two (notes: f g  a  g  f  e  f). Then, play a scale — again on the mouthpiece — making pitches really in tune with each other.

**Trombone**  Basically the same thing for the Trombone. I would try to start with the pitch. I think that pitch is so very important so you know what pitch is in your head and relate it to the embouchure. Remember, when you're warming up, you're working on not only your lip and face muscles, but the breathing muscles (rib cage and diaphragm). Take a lot of air in, blowing air through the mouthpiece. 4th line 'f' is a good note to start on. (Use your Trombone to find that f, then work on the mouthpiece only.) You can also play any melody you like. Then start to relate your pitches to the instrument, usually just long tones, similar to what the scales are.

**Horn**  The horn player first of all finds the horn pitch and then uses the mouthpiece to do patterns, breathing as often as necessary, using lots of air. Then go to the horn after the lip feels it's responding and play a pattern such as this: c d c e c f c g c a c b c c  c; *then*: c g c e g e c g  c e g e g e c. When the student becomes more familiar with the horn, use all the various fingerings starting with an open F horn, second valve, first valve, first and second together, second and third together in those same patterns. Horn players must make sure that their hand does not close off the bell; otherwise they'll be tuning to a false pitch. The hand position should be as open as possible in order to give a good clear sound and not change the pitch.

**Tuba**  We should say that the warm-up does not have to start when you are in a room with your instrument. Carry the mouthpiece around with you during the day. It's great fun on a school bus . . .

**Trumpet**  So we're creating air, lip and sound motion, and we're playing a basic pattern, a scale pattern in a nice relaxed way using lots of air and varying the dynamics. If you can only play loudly, try to get the vibration going in the mouthpiece and play softly down and up. Make like a fire siren, but slowly.

**Trumpet**  In order to get the trumpet to sound properly, a good sound on the mouthpiece is necessary. Then the sound on the instrument will also be clear. So train your ear in pitch and try to get the best tone that you can. We're back to Tone and Tuning!

**Tuba**  So far, I haven't heard anything that isn't similar. Maybe we need some different technique for the Tuba. We should stress that the Tuba player should *not* try to keep up with the players of smaller instruments insofar as breath phrases. He shouldn't try to make a long phrase. That's why I've given him twice as many breath marks in the book. As soon as you are out of air, take a breath. There is no award for duration. It is important to take a deep breath in and *get rid of it*. A nice big buzz. As soon as you are out of air, even for two quarter notes, take another breath.

**Trombone**  But, that's true, in proportion for all the other brass players. You need air to make a really rich vibrant sound. What happens is that so many students starve for air, close off, and make the sound smaller. And there goes the Tone!

**Trumpet** But the section on breathing follows. Let's show another mouthpiece exercise which in a way sums up the others. Using your mouthpiece, start on a Concert B♭ (c on a trumpet, f on a French Horn), play up a fifth (Trumpet: c d e f g f e d c). Then move up one note and repeat the exercise. Keep moving the bottom note up one note until you are at your fifth note in your beginning scale. Then, you have enough notes to play a whole octave – plus one note – on your mouthpiece. Do this in eighth notes when you can, with definite pitches, recognizable as a scale.

**Trumpet** So what we're saying is: Use your instrument to find beginning pitch, then warm up on your mouthpiece, using lots of air, gradually increasing your range, and playing definite pitches.

And a little tip: get your whole group to play the piece you're working on *just on the mouthpiece*. Make the pitches true. You eliminate many instrumental problems and can concentrate on Tone and Tuning.

**Trombone** If you have a rhythmic problem, work it out on your mouthpiece, individually or as a group. We do it all the time.

**Tuba** Buzz the mouthpiece and play two or three or more bars just on the mouthpiece, and then back on the horn. You'll immediately hear a change in the sound; it will be richer and fuller. *Sing* your parts with the group to help in tuning; then back to the horn. Keep moving from mouthpiece, singing, and to the horn. The pitch, everything, is established right there, right at the mouthpiece. The instrument simply reflects the sound we're making. It amplifies it. The embouchure (your whole face) with your mouthpiece, and your ear – that's the important thing.

# Breathing

It is very important that the student sit away from the back of the chair. SIT UP, NOT SIT DOWN! You should be sitting straight, but not rigidly straight. Lean forward just a little bit, take a deep breath and then, very easily, blow it out through your mouthpiece.

You should think that you are being held up by a hair from the top of your head – an imaginary hand is holding you up as you sit lightly on that chair, nice and erect.

We breathe in – a total breath. Not only is the chest expanding, the lungs filling up with wind, there may even be expansion and movement on the sides and back. Now breathe in and out slowly with the other members of the group, listening to them, and breathing together. 'The group that breathes together, plays together!' So now we have everyone breathing together, expanding and supporting. With your eyes closed, you should be able to hear and sense the other members of the group who are about to play a note, so that the attack is together with the air support together. Breathe in through the sides of your mouth and blow through the mouthpiece.

Think of the air column – not as the beam from a flashlight broadening drastically as it lengthens, but as a laser beam – focused, firm and alive. Keep your shoulders down, expand with the air coming in. The diaphragm drops, the ribs expand out, and the air is then supported and expelled as if your chest is a giant bellows.

If you are in doubt as to the muscles to be used for breathing, watch your dog or cat while it is sleeping. Expansion in the lower chest cavity is obvious. We've never seen a dog raise his shoulders when taking in air! So don't you. It only decreases the air capacity, tightens the throat muscles, and allows no support for the air. Besides, it looks funny!

# Tonguing

Simply: "The tip of the Tongue to the Top" say 10 times.

Tonguing is articulation of notes, defining the beginning and attack. With rare exceptions (#4, #12, #13), the tonguing should be clean but smooth (legato). After saying the line above, follow your tongue to the place on the hard palate above the front teeth. Use that spot and say "Ta". This basic tonguing will suffice, and give a clear presentation.

The simple but important exercise of practicing "ta, ta, ta," can be accomplished when riding on a bus, sitting in a bathroom, or reading a book. Concentrate on only the TIP of your tongue contacting the palate. When rehearsing with your mouthpiece, make sure your tongue stays in its place, and does NOT move down between your teeth. You're on your way to clean, bright articulation!

# Scales

Always practise the Scale of your piece playing the scale as musically as you can, producing your best TONE. Variations of Rhythm, Volume, and Breathing will help.

TRUMPETS

FRENCH HORN

TROMBONE

TUBA

PATTERNS for scales related to selections. We have only given three. Students will invent.

etc.

Suitable for 6.

etc.

Suitable for 10.

etc.

Suitable for 12.

# Hosanna

PALESTRINA

Scale: 1.

Palestrina was born near Rome, Italy about 1525. He began his musical training as a choirboy at the age of seven. Soon, he was recognized for his talent and was sent to a choir school in Rome. At the age of nineteen, he was appointed organist and choirmaster at the Cathedral in his home town. From then, until he died in 1594, he wrote Church music, attempting at a smoothness and beauty of sound rather than forceful expression.

*Hosanna* is a very simple example of his music. Notice the different styles between the opening and bar 16. The final six bars gives you an early introduction to 'imitation' — a melody repeated at different intervals in the different voices. We will see more of this in the next three selections, culminating in fugal imitation by Bach. Try to play *Hosanna* as smoothly as you can, tuning constantly.

---

Strive for a smoothness and blend of all the instruments. Re-work breathing into shorter phrases for the Tbne and Tuba if they are unable to do this themselves. Their instructions suggest that they take air when necessary without destroying the singing phrases. Since the music was written for choir, the natural musical sentence is much longer than a young Tuba player can manage. Insist on Tuning, by repeating chord by chord, listening, taping, singing, buzzing.

Editor

---

# Non Nobis Domine

BYRD

Scale: 3.

William Byrd was born in England in 1543 and lived 80 years, composing music for the Church. Queen Elizabeth I was the ruler during most of his working life; Champlain explored America before Byrd died. He survived two Church 'reformations' and was not persecuted because his music was so valued. He was considered by many as the greatest composer of the 'Elizabethan' period. He wrote for choirs and keyboard instruments.

*Non Nobis Domine* is a famous 'Canon', in three parts with the melody unchanged from the unison, the fifth, and the octave. The word 'canon' means 'rule' and is a very strict imitation of the first voice. As such, you must play this piece with the same phrasing and smoothness in all three parts. If you wish to repeat (go *around* again) then stop at the asterisk (*) and go immediately to your first note, ignoring the preceding rest(s). Conclude at the double bar.

---

Following their instructions, start the group all on their first note and play together, (2nd Tpt and F.H. a fourth lower, Tbne and Tuba in Octaves). This is the time to do the phrasing, dynamics, shape. Sing the CANON all together, then in the three parts as written. Concern yourself with pitch but not what octave range they sing in. Then, put together. This piece makes an excellent 'Chorale' tuning piece for warm-up the entire year.

Editor

---

# 1. Hosanna!

Palestrina
(1525-1594)

## 2. Non Nobis Domine

W. Byrd
(1543-1623)

This is a CANON at the 5th and 8ve.
If you wish to repeat, (go around again,) then stop at the asterisk mark (*) and go immediately to your first note, ignoring the preceding rest (s). Conclude at the double bar.

# The Silver Swan

GIBBONS

Scale: 1.

Orlando Gibbons was born in England in 1583. He received his early musical training as a choirboy in King's College, Cambridge. He was considered a great choral and keyboard composer of the late Elizabethan period. He died in 1625 while he was organist of Westminster Abbey.

*The Silver Swan* is a classic and well-known example of his madrigals. Imitation was common in the contrapuntal writing of this time, and Gibbons was the master. Throughout the selection, there is imitation in all five voices, but it is not obvious. We have 'graphed' the parts below. Find your own part and follow it closely in your music. Colour your own line; then look for similar shaped phrases in the other four parts. You will find at least ten! When you perform this piece, be aware of the imitation.

Rhythm can be a problem here. Have students clap rhythm, noting when they are teamed together, and where the imitation is. The piece is divided into two sections; learn separately, certainly on different days. When performing, draw musical attention to opposite motion of 1st Tpt and Tuba at opening. Try for a real singing tone, with the imitation apparent in the performers.

Editor

# 3. The Silver Swan

Gibbons
(1583-1625)

## Exercise: 'Imitate' Each Other

# Intrada
# A fanfare

PEZEL

Scale: 4

Johann Pezel was born in Germany in 1639. He was a professional trumpet player himself, and wrote music for Brass Ensemble. The Fanfare is a good example of his characteristic brass writing and sophisticated use of rhythmic and chordal contrasts.

A good tonguing exercise from beginning to end. Get a clean articulation that makes each note ring. Review tonguing with students. Pay close attention to dynamic range in performing and have students exaggerate. Vary dynamics in repeat sections. Here is a good time for students to try their own initiative. When ready for performance, move your group to an accoustical hall (Church, Gym, large Washroom), spread them apart, slow the tempo down and have them make a real fanfare of the Pezel.

Editor

# 4. Intrada-A Fanfare

Pezel
(1639-1694)

# Fugue in E♭

### BACH

Scale: 3.

Johann Sebastian Bach was born in Germany in 1685. His work represents the culmination in music up to his death in 1750. The imitation and canon that we have seen so far, all led to the 'Fugue'. The word 'Fugue' in French means 'flight'. This suggests that the opening part presents the melody (subject) then 'flies' before the following voices as they present the subject. Counterpoint, the interweaving of melodies, is the basis of all imitation, and ultimately, the fugue. Now, if you want to really understand what we have said, learn this simple, undeveloped fugue. Why not start with all players playing the first two bars of their own part at the same time, forgetting preceding rests. Now, you have the subject (melody). Then, learn the last 7 bars together. Now, start at the pick-up to bar 13. When all is in place, begin at the beginning, and put all the pieces together. Whenever you have the subject, you become the dominant part, and the other players support you; otherwise, you support the subject presented by the others. The climax of the piece is the Tuba entry (right, Chuck?) leading to the conclusion of the Fugue. (A good example of a more complex Fugue is to be found on our records: *Fugue in G minor* (Little) by Bach. See if we keep the subject in mind and in front of you always.) Have fun!

---

Instructions for the students in beginning this work are included in the notes above. A key point in preparing a fugue is the essential equality of Subject performance by all instruments. Your next problem: the Countersubject must support, but not be sublimated by the Subject. Originally for keyboard, this simple fugue should *sing* itself along at a good pace, with the Subject being passed from one to another like a double reverse in football.

Editor

---

# 5. Fugue in E♭

Bach
(1685-1750)

# 'Air' from Water Music

## HANDEL

Scale: 1.

George Friedrich Handel was also German, born in 1685 like Bach, but spent most of his musical life in England as the court musician for George III (who himself was German!). Handel and Bach are a curious pair: Bach reflected the past and brought it to the peak; Handel knew the past, used it, but projected more into the future. He also lived nine years longer, travelled much more, and made much more money.

The 'Air' is a simple, melodic movement from a Suite that Handel composed for the King of England. It was to provide nice background music as the King sailed down the Thames River through London in 1717. You will notice the immediate difference from #1 – 5 in this book. Handel's music is more dominant in the top and bottom part, rather than equally voiced. The melody is very important. Try to play the dotted notes longer and the following notes shorter than you think they should be. Mathematically, they must be 3:1 ratio. This selection will provide you and your audience with a great deal of satisfaction, representing as it does Handel at his finest.

---

Read the 'Learning Our Math – Lesson One in Students' Book. The major point is the common error of playing a dotted eighth-sixteenth in a ratio of 2:1, rather than 3:1,.

Note small ensembles – bar 5, F.H., Tbne, Tuba, also bar 23. Develop a new balance and blend, with the F.H. projecting, and the Tbne broadening his tone – bar 19 1st and 2nd Tpts. and F.H. Re-develop a new balance with the F.H. understanding that he is now the Tuba – the Foundation for tuning and the tonic focal point.

The 2nd Tpt part has been somewhat changed in bars 2, 14, 20 and 32 to eliminate entry on the second beat. If there is no problem for your player, feel free to re-write giving him a quarter rest and quarter note, rather than the half note. Experience has shown that a less competent player will enter roughly, and with an accent which is *not* wanted; hence, the editing.

The final performance (after much work) should be very flowing and smooth. Take notice of the Handelian Cadence, especially at pick-up to bar 35. There, an Allargando is in order, the tempo being changed for the first time in the selection. Try to develop a feeling for the colour of the instrumentation as it changes from section to section. Watch the doubling of the Tpts in bar 35 for tuning. This is a good opportunity for the 3rd valve tuning slide lesson. Dynamics, outside of the bare outline that has been presented, could be discussed and formulated by the students. The structure of the piece allows for this. I would suggest that the students listen critically to several recordings of the AIR, including the Canadian Brass recording. A good Handelian style of performance should emerge.

Editor

# 6. 'Air' from Water Music

Handel
(1685-1759)

**22** 'Air' from Water Music *continued*

**29**

# Ave Verum

MOZART

Scale: 3.

Wolfgang Amadeus Mozart was born in Austria in 1756, six years after the death of Bach. Music had progressed in many different directions since the culmination of Bach and the development of Handel. The selection presented here is not typical, on the surface, of Mozart, but in depth, is one of his simplest but finest creations using the limited resources of choir, rather than the extensive resources of the now-developed instrumental ensemble. Mozart was a child prodigy – that is, an extraordinary person who at the age of four composed the world's best known song: *Twinkle, Twinkle Little Star!*

'Ave Verum' was written very late in Mozart's life as he contemplated life following death. The work should be played with a sense of dignity, slowly, and with a full tone. This is a marvellous selection for a real concentration on tuning, tone and balance, the three real ingredients for good ensemble playing. We have included this example over all others of Mozart because of the sheer beauty of its line, harmony and shape. Most of Mozart's music seems much lighter, but all is very hard to perform in proper style. This selection plays into your hearts and flows with its own dignity. We think that you will like it.

---

There are no performance tips in the students' books here. (The answer to their crossword puzzle is given below.) Most of the words in the puzzle relate to a performance of Ave Verum. This is the one selection in the entire collection, where a *great deal* of leadership and performance preparation must be given. Again, long breath phrases – musical sentences – predominate, and care must be taken to follow the sense of the phrases faithfully. The first trumpet should present his part almost as a trumpet solo, with accompaniment from the other four voices, until bar 30, when duets between the two Tpts, and the F.H. and Tbne provide the sound colour. The 1st Tpt solo effect continues again at '37' to the end. A lightness, a well-tuned chordal structure integrated with linear clearness must pervade in order to bring the simplicity of Mozart to the fore.

Editor

---

# 7. Ave Verum

Mozart
(1756-1791)

**28** Ave Verum *continued*

# Ave Maria

### RACHMANINOFF

Scale: 1.

Sergey Rachmaninoff was born in Russia in 1873. He was educated musically through the piano and later in life was also considered an excellent orchestral conductor. Even though he died in 1943, not many years ago, his music is considered as belonging to the nineteenth century. He met Tschaikovsky when he was fifteen years old, when Tschaikovsky was 48 and only 5 years from death.

*Ave Maria* (Hail, Mary, Mother of God) is one of the few well-known choral pieces by Rachmaninoff. It is a fascinating and very powerful statement of music, utilizing the techniques of the Romantic composers in building surely and carefully to an emotional climax, while still reflecting almost the classical period of choral writing.

Let's look at the composition in depth. It opens in a very clear but thin 'texture' — a duet of the two trumpet parts. They must sound as one but in thirds. The horn joins and complements the other two, adding also a tonal colour needed for a greater depth. The trombone enters on a descending passage and creates four-part harmony, which immediately disintegrates into moving thirds between horn and 2nd Tpt, while the Trombone and 1st Tpt, in octaves, start a new melody. Any climax is built on tension, and we are now past the opening lyrical phrases and into the body. Notice that the breathing and phrasing between the two components is quite different, starting at bar 15 and carrying on until the Tuba entry at bar 21. The strongest melody is presented by the Tuba, doubled by the French Horn, while the Trumpets and Trombone continue with the previous thought. Do you realize that this is characteristic of the counterpoint of the 16th and 17th century that was discussed in numbers 1-4 of this book? The *'Ave Maria'* comes to a tranquil conclusion with a simple almost puritanical chordal structure for the last four bars. What an interesting study of texture, counterpoint, and climaxes all within 28 bars and 1½ minutes! Try to sense the emotion.

---

There is an analysis in the notes above; students should read and relate to their music. The Math lesson attempts to illuminate the major performance problem here. When two instruments are playing in thirds, or in octaves, the lower must be stronger in order to be equal. Tuning is also critical, but the piece affords excellent opportunities to overcome difficulties due to its structure. Don't 'spare the whip' on the Tuba part at 21. Your students will find this a very satisfying piece to learn and to perform.

Editor

---

# 8. Ave Maria

Rachmaninoff
(1873-1943)

By permission of Boosey and Hawkes (Canada) Ltd., Toronto

# Cwm Rhondda

WELSH

Scale: 1.

Wales is a 'state' of Britain. The Britons were defeated by the English many centuries ago, and were pushed to the far West coast of the Island. There, they kept to many of their own traditions, language, and pace of life. A need for energy developed following the Industrial Revolution, and coal mines were opened in Wales. The local workers found solace in their long dangerous hours in the pits by singing and harmonizing Hymn tunes. *Cwm Rhondda* is the most famous of all these songs.

---

We are now half-way through our book, and it seems like a great place to "re-capitulate our exposition" — to re-state our objectives and develop your thinking further.

**Tone:** The 'sound' that we make must not be forgotten as we get into more complicated notes, fingerings or rhythms, or as our range becomes extended. A player with poor tone is a player not to be enjoyed by the audience.

**Tuning:** Again, as range is extended in the next few selections, tuning becomes more important. The support of the air column, the speed and intensity of the air column will support the tone, and allow you careful tuning.

**Balance:** The next few arrangements create balance problems which can be overcome with careful listening. *Cwm Rhondda* appears so simple, but is an excellent exercise in all three areas above.

**Blend:** We have purposely not mentioned Blend earlier. The counterpoint in the music called for a more characteristic sound of the individual instrument than the individual instrument 'blending' into the ensemble. But, when we are performing 'harmonic' music, chordal music, we want to create more of a Blend — five people with one sound rather than five separate sounds. This is achieved through listening, thinking together, and the attempt to make one sound out of four distinctly different instrumental sounds.

**Rhythm:** Further, you will find: *Bones,* and the first of *Three Newfoundland Folksongs.* Each has a driving forward, pulsating rhythm that must sound as one. Be careful with your *Timing* of notes and rests; try to think as one player, not as many individuals. Sense the motion.

**Colour:** Each instrument has its own colour, determined by the construction: a Trumpet and Trombone are two-thirds cylindrical, one-third conical; therefore the tone is more focused and brighter. The French Horn (with a different overtone series — ask your teacher) and the Tuba are more conical; therefore the tone is more mellow, more singing. The second of the *Three Newfoundland Folksongs* gives the French Horn a chance to emphasize its characteristics.

The *Farewell Anthem* demands from all a smooth singing quality, especially in the overlapping of parts. The accents in *Bones* are better suited to the focused sound of the Trumpets and Trombones, but all instruments must participate in the dynamic effect. Bring your own colour to your group, but do not let the individuality of your instrument or you conflict with the unity of the whole. The Finale *Three Newfoundland Folksongs* provides all of you with a challenge in each of the six areas above. Enjoy yourself!

# 9. Cwm Rhondda

Welsh

# Carol of the Bells

UKRAINIAN

Scale: 2 (but related MINOR)

A peal of bells is heard, faintly, now getting closer, now fading away. The Tuba acts as the big and constant 'Bonger', while the other four voices take turns presenting the short subject /—/, /—/, /—/, /—/. Whenever you play that rhythm, present it exactly as your group has decided, so that it is constant. The other melodies support it, never dominating.

---

The basic teaching area here is to create a bell-sound from all the instruments. Use the scale for variety, with different rhythms to keep interest, but persevere until the bell sound begins to be heard. Try to set a model for your students with the use of records: obviously I recommend the Canadian Brass series, especially as a model for Tone and Tuning.

Editor

# 10. Carol of the Bells

Ukrainian

**29** Carol of the Bells *continued*

**37**

# El Yivneh Hagalil

ISRAEL

Scale: There is no tonic scale, as the music comes from a period long before tonality. Modes preceded tonic scales. The Mode of EL YIVNEH is: Me Fah Se Lah Te Lah
(Intervals in Step) ½ 1 ½ ½ 1
*Fah* should feel very flat; *Se* should feel very sharp.

*El Yivneh Hagalil* (The Lord will build a new Galilee) is a work song of the fields. Notice the strong rhythm when all the instruments are put together. This is a cumulative song in that parts are added in each verse. Following the Tuba part in *Carol of the Bells,* it seems appropriate to draw your attention to the Tuba solo! Here is the construction:
Tuba; Tuba & Tbne; Tuba, Tbne & Horn; Tuba, Tbne, Horn & 2nd Tpt; Tuba, Tbne, Horn, Tpts.

---

Tuba solo with simple accompaniment. Tuba player has been instructed to prepare his part separately, as the other four parts are not as demanding. This piece is a great crowd pleaser, especially when performed quite quickly and with real drive. In this, as in ALL OTHER SELECTIONS, doubling of parts (or more, for that matter) works well. Come off hard and fast – right off the end.

Editor

## 11. El Yivneh Hagalil

36

# 12. Bones

Spiritual

**63** Bones *continued*

# 13. Three Newfoundland Folksongs

Canadian

**36** Three Newfoundland Folksongs *continued*

**45** Quickly

**56** Presto

# 14. The Lord Bless You and Keep You

Peter Lutkin
(1858-1931) U.S.A.

(Farewell Anthem)

Slowly ♩=69

1st Tpt.

2nd Tpt.

F. Hn.

Tbn.

Tuba

8 The Lord Bless You and Keep You *continued*

## 15. My Country, Tis of Thee/God Save the Queen

1st Tpt.

2nd Tpt.

F. Hn.

Tbn.

Tuba

8

# 16. O Canada!

Lavallée

# A 'note' on performance

*Music* is an 'outward and visible sound of an inward and spiritual grace'. It's a joy for the individual though requiring much private practice. When brought to a group i.e. Brass Quintet, it is to be shared with the other players, just as they share with the individual. Careful attention to all detail will result in a unity of sound and thought within a social interaction.

Our music can now be shared with others — an audience. This is the true joy of performance. But certain new ideas must be kept in mind.

Programming: Choose numbers from this book or your repertoire which reflect different styles, different keys, different moods and dynamics.

| | | |
|---|---|---|
| *Example A:* | Hosanna | Palestrina |
| Easy | Intrada | Pezel |
| | Cwm Rhondda | Welsh |
| | My Country/God Save the Queen | |
| *Example B:* | The Silver Swan | Gibbons |
| Medium | Fugue in E$^b$ | Bach |
| | El Yivneh Hagalil | Israeli |
| | Three Newfoundland Folksongs | Canadian |
| *Example C:* | Air (from Water Music) | Handel |
| Difficult | Carol of the Bells (anytime) | Ukrainian |
| | Ave Maria | Rachmaninoff |
| | Bones | Spiritual |

Don't be afraid of using *O Canada*. Though it is the Anthem of Canada, it is also a good melody and will complement any programme.

Or, mix Easy, Medium and Difficult pieces to suit yourself and your audience. The listeners are not present to hear technical achievement; they want a pleasant selection of music. The good performer never allows the audience to notice technical difficulties, so choose music well within the group's capabilities.

The performance begins as you enter and finishes when you leave. Be aware of all visual details and keep distraction to a minimum.

We have constantly stressed the enjoyment of the Brass medium and the music. Try to convey this to your audience. It is infectious, and will bring real pleasure to them. Above all, enjoy yourself!

See you in the Concert Hall!

The Canadian Brass

(Next step: Volume Two — Book of Quintets)